FRANKIE THE BUNNY

MYSTERY IN THE FOREST

by Dorothy Jasnoch

Illustrations and Story - Dorothy Jasnoch
Editor - Samson O. Korzeniowski
Assistant Editor/Social Media - Ylona Cupryjak
Creative Art Director - Teodozja C. Rawicka
Multimedia Designer - Jose A. Saldivar

For information contact:
Owl About Books Publisher, Inc.
P.O. Box 897 Joshua, TX 76058
www.owlaboutbooks.com

Library of Congress Control Number: 2011943634
ISBN: 978-1-937752-01-9
Printed in the United States of America

First Edition

In memory of
Samson O. Korzeniowski
our beloved editor...

To our very special friend, Janet Busbey Nilsson, for lending her
literary expertise which greatly benefited our stories...

Ben the bear decided to clean his house and fold his freshly laundered clothes.

"I can't wait for my friends to come by later for treats!" he said happily to himself.

Ideas for desserts flowed through his head like sweet melting icing.

"So many wonderful snacks I could serve my guests," Ben thought to himself. "Most like veggies ... a lot! Oh, but I served those the last time my forest friends visited," he fussed regretfully.

"Maybe sweet things this time! I have a lot of honey to sweeten most anything I make ... But, I must choose, and get started quickly," Ben thought.

Ben went over the thoughts in his head. "Honey custard? Maybe honey and blueberry cake? Perhaps it would be better if..."

Ben was suddenly interrupted by the sound of urgent knocking at the door.

"Who might that be?" he wondered aloud.
He dashed to open the door as fast as he could.

It was Buzz the bumblebee!
Buzz seemed quite upset.

"Ben, Ben! Come quickly!" she exclaimed. "I have to show you something...something strange, something that does not belong in the forest!"

Buzz then flew off, not thinking about just how quickly a bumblebee could fly.

"Buzz is so fast!" poor Ben gasped between racing breaths. He did his best to keep up with his excited bumblebee friend.

For many minutes Ben scrambled to keep up with the quick bumblebee. He was running so fast, he didn't see the round metal object that was lying on the ground until it was too late.

Poor Ben hit the object with his foot and let out a loud, painful cry. He almost lost his balance!

"Aaaaargh! It hurts, it hurts, it hurts!" Ben whined sorrowfully. "Oh, w-w-what was that?!?!" Buzz heard Ben's cries and hurried back.

"What happened?" she asked worriedly.

"It's my foot! It hurts!" Ben whimpered. "I think I cut it!"

"Oh no!" Buzz exclaimed. "Did you step on something?"

Buzz had never seen her strong friend look so frightened and unhappy. Then, she suddenly saw the metal object that Ben had run into, hurting his foot.

"Look over there!" she cried. "Something is shining in the grass, over there!" Buzz motioned toward a clump of grass where a round, metal object glistened.

Both Buzz and Ben were in awe. What was that?

And so a mystery began for them.

Buzz remembered that this wasn't the first time a strange object has been seen in the forest. A similar object had been seen at a nearby stream a while back.

Were these two similar objects from two different places related? Was there a connection? What might it be?

"This is what I wanted to show you," Buzz said anxiously. "But I don't think you're able to walk." Buzz began to circle overhead.

"Wait here," Buzz said. "I'll go get Flutter the butterfly. We will bring you a bandage and something we can use to clean your wound."

Ben sat waiting nervously, as the others were gathering medical supplies for him. It wasn't long before Blaze the fox and Flutter the butterfly came to his rescue, alongside Buzz.

"Thank you for coming so quickly," Ben said gratefully to his friends, as they took care of him. "We'll wrap up your paw carefully and then we can see this mystery!" they all decided.

The group then took a closer look at the strange object. Everyone agreed it was the first time they had ever seen something like this. Buzz thought she had possibly seen one somewhat similar, but wasn't quite sure now.

"Have you seen anything like this?" Buzz asked Flutter curiously.

Flutter shook her head. "No, I haven't. But I know someone who could help us with this mystery. Let's visit Clarisse, the wisest of owls! She knows almost everything from reading lots of books!" Flutter said admiringly.

A journey to see Clarisse, the wisest of owls, would certainly clear up this mystery!

"Knock, knock! Greetings, Clarisse!" the animals all chimed in cheerfully when they reached the wise owl's house. "We have found something strange in the forest. Could you help us find out what it is?"

The animals brought out the metal object to show the owl.

Clarisse calmly put on her glasses. "Let me see," she answered, and held up the shiny, metal cylinder in the air. "Hoo, hoo...Can you believe it?" Clarisse exclaimed. 'It is a can!"

The animals were surprised and confused.

"A...c-a-n? A can?" The animals repeated.

"Yes, a can," replied the owl. "People keep food or drinks in them. They are very common containers for many things that people keep stored in their homes. They can't always get their food fresh like we do."

The animals were still confused.

"So, why is it in the forest?"

Everyone waited curiously for the answer. Maybe, whoever brought it and left it behind had been hungry. But, he was forgetful, too!

"Ben cut his foot on it!" Buzz exclaimed sadly. "Cans should not be left lying around the forest like that! They should be put someplace where no one can get hurt!"

Clarisse agreed with a wise nod.

"Yes, they should be put in recycling bins. Cans like this can also be processed in a factory and be made into other things."

"That's what we need to do! We need to recycle them," Ben replied, determined as ever.

The animals all thanked Clarisse for her help, and then left to go towards the stream. They all agreed they needed to get Frankie the bunny to join their adventure!

Soon all the animals reached the stream, and began to dig up and clear away any cans they could find.

By afternoon, all the cans were collected and taken to be put into recycling bins. Their job was done, but they couldn't help but wonder...

"Clarisse said that if we recycle all the cans, they could be made into new products. I bet that means we all have just saved a lot of earth's metals", Buzz mused just loud enough for the others to overhear.

Hearing this, each animal's face lit up. Each had a special good feeling about cleaning and recycling what shouldn't be left in the forest.

"Now we can walk safely in the forest," Blaze said, finally taking a deep breath of fresh clean forest air.

"We can run safely, too," added Ben happily. Then he suddenly remembered about the desserts he had been planning to make that morning. "Who thinks it's a good time for... pudding? Is anyone hungry?" he asked his friends excitedly. "We can have pudding and honey."

"Oh, yes! That sounds wonderful!" the other animals exclaimed. "Let's go!"

"Hooray for Ben!" shouted Frankie.

"Hooray for ALL of US!" added Ben.

But then Ben remembered he wasn't able to cook the pudding earlier. He didn't have time! He suddenly felt ashamed. There was nothing to eat, no dessert to enjoy. Oh, goodness!

Suddenly he realized that there was plenty of honey, however.

"Would you all like some honey, with honey, instead?" Ben asked sheepishly.

Everyone burst into laughter.

"We're with you because we're your friends, not because of treats!" his friends said cheerfully. "Everything you make is delicious, so don't fret. Let's see what we can come up with!"

Ben was truly grateful for his friends, and so he proposed a toast.

"Here's a toast to my wonderful friends, and to the wonderful forest that provides for us!" Ben cried joyfully with a big smile.

"Hur-r-ray!" all his friends responded in kind by lifting their cups of honey for this toast. In spite of occasional problems, life was good and even better when you shared things with your caring friends.

All the while, Frankie the bunny felt so happy and grateful with his company of new friends. His days of having been left behind were gone; he was now looking forward to new adventures instead...

Friends to the end,
even on the mend!

Frankie the Bunny

Ben the Bear

Blaze the Fox

Bluise the Bird

Buzz the Bumblebee

Flutter the Butterfly

Hank the Hedgehog

Stan the Snail

See if you can find all the characters in this book

FUN FACTS

Bear – The female bear will hibernate all winter long, not even waking up to give birth.

Bees – Bees can see all the colors except for red.

Bluebirds – These delightful songbirds readily accept food from nest boxes.

Butterfly – These creatures have tongues almost as long as their bodies.

Fox – A fox can hear a watch ticking from 40 yards away!

Hedgehog – By curling into a tight ball and tucking in their heads, tail, and legs, they protect the softer parts of their bodies that don't have spines.

Rabbit – A boy rabbit is called a 'buck' and a girl rabbit is called a 'doe.' Rabbits can produce 20-40 babies in a year, but require lots of exercise each day. Their bones can break easily otherwise.

Snail – Snails have soft bodies and can hide in a hard shell. Snails can go three months without food!

About the Author

Dorothy Jasnoch, author and illustrator of childrens' books, has written a colorful and deeply meaningful series of stories - "Frankie the Bunny and his friends".

The author and her series are the winners of the European competition "Fairytale World in non-Fairytale Reality". Following this success, "Frankie the Bunny" was published in cooperation with the European Foundation for Child-Victims of Road Accidents and the "Return" Foundation in Jantar, Poland, 2008, raising thousands of dollars to assist in the treatment of childhood disabilities.

The books have proven a great success for the author and joy for the readers.

The heroes of the stories are the animals from both healthy and "unhealthy" worlds, who by forming the closest cordial ties, show that there is only one world: the world of friends with open hearts. Compassion, helpfulness and dedication to each other are their only super-power. The stories, though, for children carry a deep spiritual and integration message and can be enjoyed by both parents and children together. It is an excellent book to pass quality time and learn.The heroes break seemingly unbreakable boundaries frequently covered by the sanctity of taboos.

The author and illustrator, who lives in Texas with her inspirations- her two children, her husband, a cat and a dog, using characters and narrative logical to children, cleverly depict the world of adults they will one day be a part of. Animated illustrations accompanied by subtle but vibrant narrative gently take the reader inside the heart of the story. It is a timeless journey with a chance to enjoy and reflect.

It would mean the world to Frankie if you would like to be his friend; he surely wants to be yours. Making you smile makes him happy.

CPSIA information can be obtained
at www.ICGtesting.com
Printed in the USA
LVIC04131060712

289053LV00004B